ANTONIO SPINELLO

ChatGPT
Beginner to Pro

Learn the basics of AI, unleashes its power, boost your earnings.

TABLE OF CONTENTS

- INTRODUCTION — 3

- What exactly is ChatGPT? — 7
- The basics of Natural Language Processing — 10
- Getting started with ChatGTP — 13
- Understanding the Pre-training Process — 18
- Fine-tuning ChatGPT for Specific Tasks — 23
- Techniques for Beginners using ChatGPT — 27
- Advanced Techniques for using ChatGPT — 33
- Best Practices and Troubleshooting — 38
- Real-Life Uses from People — 41
- Ideas and Uses in the Industry — 45
- AI and Chat GPT in the Healthcare — 49
- Finance: a Key for Investing? — 53
- ChatGPT and Education: a new World — 56
- Ideas and Uses in Social Networks — 59
- A new Money Machine? — 63
- Advanced Strategies for Making Money — 66
- Ethical Aspects — 70

- CONCLUSION — 73

- PROMPTS — 76

INTRODUCTION

In today's fast-paced world, technology is changing the way we live and work. One of the most exciting areas of technology today is natural language processing (NLP), which is revolutionizing the way we interact with machines and the way machines interact with us. One of the most powerful NLP models available today is ChatGPT, a large language model developed by OpenAI. It represents a first concrete meeting point between humanity and artificial intelligence.

This book provides a comprehensive tutorial on how to use ChatGPT effectively and how to develop the abilities necessary to produce text that resembles human speech, carry out activities requiring natural language understanding, and even translate languages. It covers everything, from the fundamentals of how this new software operates to advanced methods for making money with ChatGPT. It also covers how to customize it for particular areas and jobs. This book will arm you with the information and resources you need, whether you're a business or an individual, to use artificial intelligence efficiently and earn money by offering clients useful services and insights. The potential of this book is not just to provide the reader with a technical understanding of -

how the software works, but also to show the reader how this technology can be leveraged to improve their own lives and careers. ChatGPT has the potential to change the way we work, and by understanding how to use it, individuals can gain a competitive advantage in their field.

This book is aimed at anyone who wants to learn how to use ChatGPT properly, from beginners who are new to NLP to experienced professionals who want to take their skills to the next level. It covers everything from the basics of how this software works and how to fine-tune it for specific domains and tasks, to advanced strategies for making money with this powerful intelligent tool.
It also focuses on the business side of ChatGPT, showing how businesses can use this technology to improve their operations and increase their revenue. Everybody can use this AI chat to generate human-like text, perform natural language understanding tasks, and even translate languages. This can help them to improve their customer service, increase their productivity and reduce their costs.

The world is changing rapidly and ChatGPT is at the forefront of this change. This book is designed to give readers the knowledge and skills they need to use this incredible tool effectively and make money by providing valuable services and insights to clients. Whether you're a business or an individual, this book will give you the knowledge and tools you need to use ChatGPT -

effectively and make money by providing valuable services and insights to clients.

In this book we will explore the many possibilities that ChatGPT has to offer, from providing language generation services, natural language understanding services, language translation services, automated content creation services, chatbot and virtual assistant development, and data analysis and research, to creating and selling GPT-powered software and applications, offering consulting services, providing training and education services, and more.

Additionally, we will explore how ChatGPT can be used to make money, and how businesses and individuals can use this technology to improve their operations and increase their revenue. We will explore various strategies for making money with ChatGPT, such as creating and selling GPT-powered chatbot platforms, providing GPT-powered writing and editing services, offering GPT-powered virtual writing assistants, providing GPT-powered language learning services, GPT-powered search engine optimization services, GPT-powered market research services, and more.

It's suggested to use diverse and inclusive datasets when fine-tuning the model, in order to avoid biases and to ensure that the -

generated text is inclusive and respectful of different cultures and communities. Additionally, it's important to consider the ethical implications of using ChatGPT and to use it responsibly.

Overall, this book will provide a comprehensive guide on how to use ChatGPT effectively and how to make money by providing valuable services and insights to clients. It will explore the many possibilities that the software has to offer and show how businesses and individuals can use this technology to improve their operations and increase their revenue. With the right approach and the right use case, ChatGPT can be a powerful tool for businesses, organizations, and individuals to make money.

By reading it, you will gain a solid understanding of the capabilities and limitations of ChatGPT, and you'll learn how to use it responsibly and ethically. With this knowledge, you will be able to harness the power of artificial intelligence to generate human-like text, perform natural language understanding tasks, and even translate languages, and you'll be able to make money by providing valuable services and insights to clients.

CHAPTER 1

What exactly is ChatGPT?

"Language is the most massive and inclusive art we know, a mountainous and anonymous work of unconscious generations." - Edward Sapir

ChatGPT, short for "Conversational Generative Pre-training Transformer", is a state-of-the-art language model developed by OpenAI. It is a pre-trained transformer-based language model that can generate human-like text in a wide range of tasks such as text generation, language translation, and text summarization.

The model is trained on a massive dataset of text, known as the "training corpus", which is used to train the model to understand the patterns and structure of natural language text. The corpus used to train this powerful software is one of the largest in the world, containing over 570GB of text data. This allows the model to have a wide-ranging knowledge about the world and generate text about any topic, not just the ones it was fine-tuned on.

Using the unsupervised learning method known as "masked language modeling," the model is trained on the vast text dataset during the pre-training phase of ChatGPT. For example, it can be used to generate text that is coherent, fluent, -

and consistent, the model learns the patterns and structures seen in natural language text.

After the pre-training process, the model can be fine-tuned on specific tasks using transfer learning. Fine-tuning a pre-trained model like ChatGPT on a specific task involves training the model on a smaller dataset that is specific to the task at hand. This allows the model to learn the specific patterns and structures that are needed for the task, while still leveraging the knowledge it acquired during pre-training.

The model can be powerfully enhanced and customized to meet the demands of your particular project by fine-tuning it. To optimize the model's performance on the particular job, the procedure entails changing the model's parameters, such as the learning rate and the batch size. When fine-tuning the model, it's crucial to take the dataset's size and quality into account. In addition to the necessary trainer abilities, a larger and more varied dataset will enable the model to gain greater understanding of the task and enhance performance. However, it may also necessitate more computational time and resources during training.

Once the model is fine-tuned, it can be used to perform a wide range of NLP tasks. For example, it can be used to generate text that is coherent, fluent, and consistent with human-like language, which makes it useful for tasks such as text generation, language translation, and text summarization.

It can also be used to extract structured information from unstructured text data and make it more usable for further analysis or processing.

ChatGPT also has the ability to understand the context and relationships between words, which allows it to generate text that is coherent and fluent, with human-like language and answers. Therefore, it is able to generate such human-like text when fine-tuned on specific tasks such as text generation, language translation, and text summarization. The more specific and detailed the training, the better ChatGPT will work.

It's crucial to think about ChatGPT's ethical ramifications in addition to its features. Since the model is based on the data it was trained on, any biases and errors should be corrected. When perfecting the model, it's crucial to employ inclusive and diverse datasets and to consider any potential ethical ramifications of the output text.

An effective pre-trained transformer-based language model that can be applied to a variety of NLP applications is what we currently have. It can be adjusted to perform better and fit the demands of your project by being fine-tuned for particular jobs. When fine-tuning the model, it's crucial to take into account the amount and quality of the dataset and to be conscious of any potential ethical ramifications of the generated text.

CHAPTER 2

The basics of Natural Language Processing (NLP)

"AI is not going to take over the world, but it will change the world." - Yann LeCun

In this chapter, we will provide an in-depth overview of the basics of Natural Language Processing (NLP) and how it relates to ChatGPT.

NLP is a field of study that focuses on the interactions between human language and computers. It involves developing algorithms and models that can understand, interpret, and generate human-like language in a really short period of time. NLP has a wide range of applications, from automated customer service to machine translation and so on.

Understanding the meaning of text is one of the primary goals of NLP. Although it may seem obvious to many, it is not as straightforward as people believe. This can be achieved using methods like named entity recognition, which recognizes in text entities like persons, locations, and organizations, and sentiment analysis, which establishes the text's emotional tone. Because of the feelings we experience and desire to express, each of us -

actually writes in a unique way. These methods are used to extract structured data from unstructured text data and transform it into a more useable form for additional processing or analysis.

Language creation, which entails producing text that is cohesive, fluid, and consistent with human-like language, is another essential NLP activity. Text creation, text summarization, and text completion are all closely linked tasks. Language models, like ChatGPT in our case, which are trained on a sizable dataset of text data to comprehend the patterns and structure of human language, can be used to complete these tasks.

Language translation, text summarization, and text classification are further crucial NLP activities. Text summary requires condensing a text while keeping its key concepts, text classification entails categorizing texts into predetermined groups, and language translation entails transferring texts from one language to another.

ChatGPT is, then, a pre-trained transformer-based language model that is trained using the unsupervised learning technique. It's fine-tuned on specific tasks using transfer learning, which allows the model to learn faster and with less data than if it were starting from scratch.

The model is trained using a sizable text dataset known as the "training corpus" as part of ChatGPT's pre-training procedure. The model is trained using this corpus to -

recognize the patterns and structures seen in natural language text. A sizable corpus, which is frequently a collection of text data from books, journals, and websites, is used to train the model. As indicated earlier, with more than 570GB of text data, the corpus utilized to train ChatGPT is one of the biggest in the world.

NLP is a field of study that deals with the interactions between human language and computers. It involves a wide range of tasks, from understanding the meaning of text to language generation in many different fields, adapting as much as possible to the situation and the context created and suggested by the person who is using the software. This is why it is able to generate such human-like text when fine-tuned on specific tasks, being able to produce texts that are extremely similar to those produced by a human, albeit with some limitations due to the system's still limited experience.

In this chapter, we have discussed the basics of NLP, its tasks and its applications. We also introduced our incredible software, a powerful pre-trained transformer-based language model that is fine-tuned on specific tasks using transfer learning. With this knowledge, you will be able to understand the basics of NLP and how it relates to ChatGPT, which will help you to use it more effectively.

CHAPTER 3

Getting started with ChatGPT

"The limits of my language mean the limits of my world." - Ludwig Wittgenstein

In this chapter, we will explore the basics of how to use ChatGPT and some of the ways it can be used to improve your own projects or to develop your ideas.

This is a powerful language model that can be used for a wide range of natural language processing (NLP) tasks. In this chapter, we will provide an in-depth guide on how to get started with using ChatGPT for your specific NLP task.

The ChatGPT version you want to utilize must first be chosen. The two main ChatGPT versions available are the smaller "basic" version and the larger "large" version. Because the large version contains more parameters than the base version, which has fewer parameters and is better suited for occupations requiring less processing power, the large version is excellent for tasks requiring more computing power.

The next step is to choose how you wish to use ChatGPT. This tool can be applied in one of two ways: as a pre-trained model or as a model that has been fine-tuned. A pre-trained model is one that has undergone masked -

language modeling—an unsupervised learning technique—training on a sizable text dataset. A pre-trained model that has been refined on a particular task using a smaller dataset is known as a fine-tuned model. As a result, it will be far more accurate and precise because it is focused at particular targets.

Once you have decided which version of this software you want to use and how you want to use it, you can begin using the model. You can use the model directly by loading the pre-trained weights or fine-tuned weights and using them to perform your specific NLP task. To use ChatGPT in a proper way, you will need to have a good understanding of the task you are trying to accomplish and the data you will be using.

For example, if you are using ChatGPT for text generation, you will need to have a dataset of text that is similar to the type of text you want to generate. If you are using ChatGPT for language translation, you will need to have a dataset of text in the language you want to translate from and the language you want to translate to, and then proceed with the commands.

Once you have your data, you can use it to fine-tune the software. Fine-tuning a pre-trained model like ChatGPT on a specific task involves training the model on a smaller dataset that is specific to the task at hand. This allows the model to learn the specific patterns and structures that are needed for the task, while still leveraging the -

knowledge it acquired during pre-training. The fine-tuning process involves adjusting the model's parameters, such as the learning rate and the batch size, to optimize its performance on the specific task.

It's also important to consider the size and quality of the dataset when fine-tuning the model. A larger and more diverse dataset will allow the model to learn more about the task and improve its performance, but it may also require more resources and time to train.

You can utilize the fine-tuned model to carry out your particular NLP task after the fine-tuning procedure is finished. The refined model can be used to create text, translate text, or extract structured data from unstructured text data, for instance.

The model is based on the data it was trained on; thus it may have biases and inaccuracies that should be addressed. It's also crucial to think about the ethical aspects of utilizing ChatGPT. When perfecting the model, it's crucial to employ inclusive and diverse datasets and to consider any potential ethical ramifications of the output text.

For a variety of NLP tasks, ChatGPT is a potent pre-trained transformer-based language model. It can be adjusted to perform better and fit the demands of your project by being fine-tuned for particular jobs. The task and the data must be well understood during the fine-tuning process, -

and the resultant text's ethical implications must be taken into account.

First, you will need to have access to the model. You can either access it through OpenAI's API or by downloading the model and running it on your local machine. Both options have their own set of pros and cons, such as the flexibility and ease of use of the API or the speed and privacy of running the model locally.

Once you have access to the model, you can try out various applications for it. Text creation is one of ChatGPT's most frequently used use cases. You can tell the model to create content based on a trigger that you provide, such a sentence or a few paragraphs.
For illustration, you can input "The model can create a continuation of this sentence like "John and Sarah had been preparing this trip for weeks and were eager to finally be on the route as the sun was lowering over the mountains as they started their journey. As they strolled, the sky's colors gradually changed, portraying the surroundings in shades of orange and pink."

Another common use case is text completion, where you can provide the model with a partially written sentence or a phrase and have it complete it. The capacity of ChatGPT to carry out linguistic operations like question answering, text summarization, and language translation is another potent feature. Although we don't have enough experience to say for sure, it appears that the program -

has a great deal of potential for doing these duties really well.

ChatGPT can be used to train and fine-tune your own models. You can enhance a pre-trained model's performance for particular tasks by tweaking it with your own dataset. This is especially helpful for jobs with little available data or for tasks that are roughly similar to the tasks the model was trained on.

In the next chapter, we will try to understand more about the Pre-training process of our software. Now that you have an understanding of how ChatGPT works, you can start experimenting with it and finding ways to use it to improve your own projects.

CHAPTER 4

Understanding the Pre-training Process

"The best way to predict the future is to invent it." - Alan Kay

In this chapter, we will delve deeper into the pre-training process of ChatGPT and understand how the model is able to generate such human-like text.

As previously mentioned, ChatGPT is a transformer-based language model that makes use of an approach called unsupervised pre-training. This indicates that the model was developed using a sizable text data set without any predetermined objective in mind. In accordance with what the user wishes to accomplish with the model, it is then optimized for a variety of tasks. The model is trained on a sizable dataset of text as part of this powerful software's pre-training phase. To train the model to recognize the patterns and structure of natural language text, a sizable dataset was used. For the purpose of training the model, the corpus is often a sizable collection of text data from books, papers, and websites.

The model is trained using a technique known as "masked language modeling" where certain words in the text are -

replaced with a special token, known as the "mask token". The model is then trained to predict the missing words based on the context provided by the surrounding words. This technique is used to train the model to understand the relationship between different words in a sentence and how they relate to each other. The model is trained to predict the next word in a sentence, given the context of the previous words.

The pre-training process is done in several stages.

First, the model is trained on a large dataset of text data, allowing it to learn the patterns and structure of natural language text. Then, the model is fine-tuned on specific tasks, and this allows the model to learn the specific patterns and structures that are needed for a particular task.

The dataset is cleaned and preprocessed to remove any irrelevant or low-quality data, and then tokenized and transformed into a format that can be used to train the model.

The pre-training process of ChatGPT is a computationally intensive task that requires a significant amount of computational resources and memory. The model is trained using a large number of GPUs and a distributed computing system. It's also important to have enough memory available to store the model and the dataset.

A pre-trained model is used as the foundation for a new task during the pre-training process utilizing a method called "transfer learning." As a result, the model may learn more quickly and with less input than it could if it had to start from zero.

When ChatGPT is fine-tuned for certain tasks, the pre-training process enables it to comprehend the patterns and structure of natural language text, which is why it can produce content that is so convincingly human-like. The model can produce text that is coherent, fluent, and consistent with human-like language since it has the capacity to comprehend word relationships and context.

It is also worth noting that the pre-training process allows ChatGPT to have a wide-ranging knowledge about the world, and it can generate text about any topic, not just the ones it was fine-tuned on.

This is possible because the model has been trained on a diverse set of text data, and it's able to generalize and adapt to new situations. This knowledge is encoded in the model's parameters, which can be fine-tuned for specific tasks.

The pre-training stage of ChatGPT is essential for the model to produce text that is human-like. The model can comprehend the patterns and structure of natural language text and comes closer to understanding emotions in many forms thanks to the usage of a large textual dataset and the masked language modeling -

technique. The model can produce consistent text in a matter of seconds thanks to this knowledge and some careful tuning for particular applications.

One of the important features that distinguishes ChatGPT from other language models is its pre-training procedure, which is also a core component of its capabilities.

Using transfer learning, the pre-trained model is then improved on particular tasks, enabling the model to learn more quickly and with less data than if it were beginning from scratch. In order to optimize the model's performance on the particular task, the fine-tuning procedure entails changing the model's parameters, such as the learning rate and the batch size.

The pre-training procedure is a crucial stage in the model's development since it enables the model to learn a variety of information about the outside world and comprehend the structures and patterns found in natural language text.

The fine-tuning process then makes use of this knowledge, enabling the model to learn more quickly and with less input.

It's important to note that the pre-training corpus used can affect the performance and the bias of the model. Also, the pre-training process is a one-time process, so it's essential to carefully consider the training corpus and preprocessing steps to ensure that the model is general enough and not biased.

In conclusion, the pre-training process of ChatGPT is a critical step in the development of the model. It involves training the model on a massive dataset of text, known as the "training corpus", which is used to train the model to understand the patterns and structure of natural language text.

The pre-training process is carried out using the unsupervised learning technique known as masked language modeling, which involves masking a percentage of the words in the training corpus and then training the model to predict the masked words, given the context of the surrounding words.

The training corpus is selected based on the diversity and quality of the data and is preprocessed and tokenized before being used to train the model.

CHAPTER 5

Fine-tuning ChatGPT for Specific Tasks

"The most important thing is to never stop questioning." - Albert Einstein

In this chapter, we will delve deeper into the process of fine-tuning ChatGPT for specific tasks and the considerations that need to be considered when doing so. Fine-tuning a pre-trained model like ChatGPT on a specific task involves training the model on a smaller dataset that is specific to the task at hand.
This allows the model to learn the specific patterns and structures that are needed for the task, while still leveraging the knowledge it acquired during pre-training.

When fine-tuning a model, it's important to choose a dataset that is representative of the task you want to perform. For example, if you want to fine-tune the model for text generation, you should use a dataset of text that is similar to the type of text you want the model to generate.
This will help the model to generate text that is coherent, fluent and consistent with the type of text you want to generate.

When perfecting the model, it's crucial to take the size of the dataset into account. The model will be able to learn more about the task and perform better with a larger dataset, but it may also take more time and computer resources to fully train due to the increased memory requirements.

On the other side, a smaller dataset will take less processing power and training time, but it might not be enough to adequately train the model.

The quantity of training steps is a crucial factor to take into account when optimizing the model. The quantity of the dataset and the difficulty of the task will determine how many training steps are necessary.

The model will be able to learn more about the task and perform better with more training steps, but it may also take longer and use more computer resources. On the other hand, lessening the number of training stages will save time and computational resources, but the model might not pick up enough new information to perform better.

When fine-tuning the model, you can also adjust the learning rate, which controls the speed at which the model learns.

A lower learning rate will result in slower learning but will also reduce the risk of the model overfitting. A higher learning rate will result in faster learning but may also increase the risk of the model overfitting. Finding the right balance between learning rate and number of training -

steps is crucial to fine-tune the model effectively.

Another important factor to consider is the parameter of the temperature. When fine-tuning the model, you can adjust the temperature parameter to control the level of creativity and randomness of the generated text. Lowering the temperature will result in more conservative and predictable text, while increasing the temperature will result in more creative and varied text.

When fine-tuning the model, it's also crucial to take your available computing resources into account. It's important to have a high-performance computer with a strong GPU, because fine-tuning a model demands a sizable amount of processing power and memory. Ample RAM must be available in order to store the dataset and the model.

The performance evaluation of ChatGPT is a crucial component in tuning the system. Perplexity, BLEU, ROUGE, and METEOR scores are just a few of the metrics that can be used to assess a language model's performance. These metrics give you the ability to gauge the model's text generation's quality and contrast it with human-written content.

As a result, improving the performance and modifying a pre-trained model like ChatGPT to the demands of your project can be accomplished by carefully tweaking it to a particular task. You may effectively and efficiently fine-tune the model by taking into account the factors -

covered in this chapter, such as the size and quality of the dataset, the number of training steps, the batch size, and the learning rate. It's also essential to keep an eye on the refined model's performance and change the parameters as necessary.

This chapter has covered the steps involved in customizing this tool for particular jobs as well as the factors that must be taken into account. With this basic knowledge, you could not try to fine-tune the model effectively and efficiently and improve its performance for your specific task.

We will now go through several beginner-friendly approaches that will make ChatGPT and its sophisticated system appear simple and approachable.

CHAPTER 6

Techniques for Beginners using ChatGPT

""To know how to suggest is the great art of teaching." - Henri Frederic Amiel

A variety of natural language processing (NLP) activities can be performed using ChatGPT, a potent language model.
Knowing where to begin when utilizing the software can be intimidating for a newcomer. We'll give an in-depth tutorial on ChatGPT techniques for novices in this chapter.

It's crucial to first comprehend the fundamentals of ChatGPT's operation. A pre-trained transformer-based language model called ChatGPT can produce text that is human-like for a variety of activities, including text generation, translation, text summarization, calculation, design, and more. The model is trained to recognize the patterns and structure of natural language text using a sizable dataset of text known as the "training corpus" (we explained it before).

You can begin playing around with ChatGPT once you have a basic knowledge of how it functions. Using the pre-trained model for text generation is one of the easiest methods for novices. By giving the pre-trained model a prompt or a seed text, you can use it to generate text. The model will then produce text based on the prompt or seed text.

This is a fantastic method to quickly produce text without having to adjust the model and get a sense for how it functions. You might start by asking general or specific questions to get a better understanding of the program and the chances and potential it offers. You can learn how the software reacts to your requests, making sure that you personalize your experience as much as possible.

Another technique for beginners is to use the pre-trained model for text summarization. You can use the pre-trained model to summarize text by providing a longer piece of text and then allowing the model to generate a shorter summary of the text. This is a great way to quickly get an overview of a piece of text without having to read through the entire thing.

It is typically advised to fine-tune the pre-trained model with a task-specific dataset for more difficult NLP tasks like language translation, text categorization, and named entity recognition. This enables the model to build on the pre-training information it already has while learning the unique patterns and structures required for the task. The model is fine-tuned by training it on a more focused dataset, which enables the model to learn more quickly -

and with less input. The dataset's size, quality, and the precise task you're seeking to complete should all be taken into account while fine-tuning the model.

Another technique for beginners is to use pre-built fine-tuned models or pre-built pipelines that are available for certain NLP tasks. These pre-built models and pipelines can be easily integrated into your projects and can save you the time and effort of fine-tuning the model yourself. You can find some just looking on platforms like Google of YouTube.

In order to use our software correctly and profitably, we must first understand how to accurately target it at a certain audience/goal.

In reality, ChatGPT tends to respond to us with answers that are either incredibly ambiguous or, at the very least, missing the actual material that we had specifically requested because it is an artificial intelligence program and not a human person. You will also frequently be told that the program cannot offer an opinion or counsel because it is not a human being, even for the most straightforward duties we can give it.

Open your computer and visit the ChatGPT website to get a better understanding of what we're talking about. After logging in, you will see a fairly straightforward interface with a space for your question at the bottom. This space will appear as soon as you do.

Giving a generic request, like "give me a title for my book on ChatGPT," will cause the software to generate a list of titles based solely on what you just said. Consequently, a very general and ambiguous query receives a similarly general and hazy response.

On the other hand, you will receive a far more thorough and unique response if you pose the question in a more particular manner, such as "Act as an author and offer me a title for my book "How does ChatGPT work?" You will have effectively directed the program in your direction and gotten the most out of it if you do it this manner.

As a powerful pre-trained transformer-based language model, ChatGPT is effective for a variety of NLP tasks. Before moving on to more difficult jobs as a novice, it can be good to start with basic strategies like text production and text summarizing. The model's performance can be enhanced by fine-tuning it using a task-specific dataset, but it's also crucial to think about the ethical ramifications of the generated text. Pre-built models and pipelines can also be used to save time and effort, but it's crucial to think about how the generated language will be perceived ethically.

Tips and Tricks for Beginners

Using ChatGPT can initially seem difficult for a newcomer. But with a few pointers and tricks, you can use this potent language model like an expert in no time. Here are some tips for maximizing the potential of ChatGPT.

- Direct the dialogue with questions: giving ChatGPT a prompt, or a place to start the conversation, is one of the most efficient ways to use it. If you're creating a script, for instance, you could give ChatGPT a list of the characters and the relationships they have, then ask it to create a scenario between them. By doing so, the model will be better able to understand your needs and produce responses that are more accurate.
- Try out various inputs: ChatGPT is a flexible model that may be used for a range of purposes. Try playing with various inputs to observe how the model responds, such as queries, statements, or even images. You'll be astonished at how well it can comprehend and produce content from various forms of input.
- Fine-tune the model for your unique task: if you're using ChatGPT for a particular task, like writing scripts or responding to inquiries, it can be useful to fine-tune the model on a dataset unique to that task. As a result, the model will be better able to understand the complexities of the task and produce correct results.

- Use ChatGPT's generated text as a jumping off point for your own writing by using the model's output as a guide. Utilize the output of the model as a starting point, then tweak and improve it to make it your own.

- Pay attention to context and how text is used: ChatGPT is a strong tool, but it's crucial to keep in mind that it can only be as effective as the input it receives. Be conscious of any potential biases or inaccuracies in the model's output and the context in which the text is being used.

Here are some sample prompts you can try using with ChatGPT in addition to these suggestions:
- Write a conversation between two people discussing a new business idea
- Generate a description of a new technology and its potential impact on society
- Write a short story about a mysterious creature living in the woods
- Create a recipe for a vegan meal
- Write a script for a scene in a detective movie

You'll be well on your way to becoming a Pro by paying attention to these suggestions and experimenting with other prompts.

CHAPTER 7

Advanced Techniques for using ChatGPT

"In the beginner's mind there are many possibilities, but in the expert's, there are the good ones." - Unknown

In this chapter, we will shortly explore some advanced techniques for using ChatGPT to improve your own projects.

One technique is fine-tuning the pre-trained model on your own dataset.
This can be useful for tasks with a limited amount of data or for tasks that are similar but not exactly the same as the tasks the model was originally trained on. Fine-tuning the model allows it to better understand and perform the specific task you are working on.

Another technique is to use the model in combination with other tools or libraries.
For example, you can use ChatGPT in combination with a sentiment analysis library to generate text with a specific sentiment or use it with a summarization library to generate a summary of a text.

You can also use the model for data augmentation, where you can set ChatGPT to generate additional examples for your dataset. This can be useful for tasks with limited data or for tasks where it is difficult to collect data. By using this skill, you can replenish your database with new examples and extend it, allowing you to get a better overview of the topic.

Utilizing the concept for interactive applications like chatbots or voice assistants is another strategy.
Real-time replies to user input can be generated using ChatGPT, enabling more believable and interesting interactions. All the chatbots on popular websites with customer support are an excellent example. With a variety of pre-configured question-and-answer alternatives, they are made to listen to and understand the customer's question before generating as coherent and pertinent an answer as they can. Naturally, this results in less work for humans and the availability of practical assistance.

Another strategy is to apply the concept to more artistic endeavors like creating poetry, fiction, or even music. The potential of ChatGPT to produce human-like prose can be leveraged to produce original and fascinating pieces of art.
However, keep in mind that, despite how brilliant the software may appear, the writing is not likely to elicit the same feelings that a human writer can, in part due to one's unique writing style.

The model can also be used to create fresh data for model training and to train other models. When you just have a small quantity of data or wish to boost the effectiveness of other models, like chatbots or other interactive systems, this can be helpful.

In the next chapter, we will explore some best practices for using ChatGPT and ways to troubleshoot common issues. By using these advanced techniques, you can take full advantage of the capabilities of ChatGPT and use it to improve your own projects in creative and innovative ways.

Tips and Tricks for Pros

As you have progressed through your journey with ChatGPT, you may have discovered that there are certain advanced techniques and strategies that can help you get even more out of this powerful language model. In this chapter, we will explore some of the best tips and tricks for pros who want to take their ChatGPT usage to the next level.

- Fine-tuning the model: you may already be aware of this but fine-tuning the model with your own unique data is one of the most effective ways to increase ChatGPT's effectiveness. To accomplish this, you can start with the pre-trained weights and train the model using your own data by employing a technique known as transfer learning. This can assist the model in picking up on your particular linguistic idioms and idiomatic expressions, which will enhance accuracy and fluency.
- Using context: ChatGPT may generate text in response to a prompt, but it can also consider the context of earlier writing. When you want to create text that carries on a dialogue or a story, or when you want to maintain a particular tone or style, this can be helpful. Simply provide the model the prior text as part of the instruction to use context.
- Using constraints: using constraints is another effective technique to manage ChatGPT's output. -

You can give the model constraints in the form of precise requirements, such as a word or phrase that must appear in the output. When you want to make sure that the model creates text that is consistent with a particular topic or theme, this can be helpful.

- Using the API: if you are planning to use ChatGPT in a production setting, it is important to use the API provided by OpenAI. This will allow you to easily integrate this software into your application, and will also provide you with additional features such as rate limiting and authentication.
- Using constraints: using constraints is another effective technique to manage ChatGPT's output. You can give the model constraints in the form of precise requirements, such as a word or phrase that must appear in the output. When you want to make sure that the model creates text that is consistent with a particular topic or theme, this can be helpful.

CHAPTER 8

Best Practices and Troubleshooting

"The goal of AI is not to mimic human intelligence but to surpass it." - Demis Hassabis

A variety of natural language processing (NLP) activities can be performed using ChatGPT, a potent language model. As with any technology, it's crucial to adhere to best practices and be ready to handle any issues that can come up when using the program.
We will give a comprehensive overview of recommended practices and troubleshooting for using ChatGPT in this chapter.

First, it's important to understand the limitations of this tool. As a pre-trained model, ChatGPT is based on the data it was trained on, so it may contain biases and inaccuracies that should be addressed. It's important to use diverse and inclusive datasets when fine-tuning the model and to be aware of the potential ethical implications of the generated text. It is also a large model, and it may require significant computational resources, memory and time to run. It's important to have a powerful machine and enough memory available to store the model and the dataset when using ChatGPT.

Monitoring the model's performance during fine-tuning and modifying the model's parameters, such as the learning rate and the batch size, to improve its performance on the job, is another excellent practice while utilizing the software. In order to prevent overfitting, it's crucial to employ strategies like early halting. It's crucial to examine the logs and error messages when troubleshooting ChatGPT problems in order to find any hints as to what the problem's root cause might be.

It's also crucial to look over the software and hardware specifications to make sure the model is being executed on a computer with suitable memory and processing power.

A common issue is model performance not meeting expectations.

This can be caused by a number of factors such as an insufficient dataset, a poor choice of fine-tuning parameters, or a lack of diversity in the dataset. In such cases, it's important to re-evaluate the dataset, try different fine-tuning parameters, and consider using techniques such as data augmentation to improve the diversity of the dataset.

Another troubleshooting tip is to try using pre-built fine-tuned models or pre-built pipelines that are available for certain NLP tasks.

These pre-built models and pipelines can be easily integrated into your projects and can save you the time and effort of fine-tuning the model yourself.

Additionally, it's critical to keep in mind that ChatGPT is a very sophisticated model, and this guide may not address difficulties that are unique to your use case. For further support and direction in these situations, it's crucial to refer to the manuals, internet sources, and the community.

It is crucial to be ready to solve potential problems and to seek out more support and advice from the community, internet sources, and documentation. You can make sure that you are using ChatGPT successfully and efficiently to enhance your own projects by adhering to these best practices and addressing frequent problems.

CHAPTER 9

Real-Life Uses from People

"AI is going to be the single most powerful force of our time." - Mark Zuckerberg

ChatGPT is a powerful language model that can be used for a wide range of natural language processing (NLP) tasks.
However, the model is not just limited to academic and research use cases, it can also be used by common people to improve their daily lives in various ways. In this chapter, we will explore some of the ideas and real-life uses of ChatGPT from common people.

Text generation is one of the most often used applications of ChatGPT among regular people. You can use ChatGPT to produce poetry, music lyrics, and many other types of writing prompts. For writers and artists trying to come up with fresh ideas or get through writer's block, this can be a great tool.
The approach can be tailored to a particular genre or writing style, such as poetry, song lyrics, fiction, non-fiction, etc. By doing this, the generated text will more closely resemble the model's refined style and be more helpful to the user. This program can also be used by -

regular individuals to create text for complete novels, blog entries, and social media updates.

Another popular use of this tool among common people is for text summarization.
ChatGPT can be used to summarize long articles, documents, and reports, making it an excellent tool for busy professionals and students who want to quickly understand the main points of a text. This can be particularly useful for people who have to read a lot of documents for work or school, and don't have the time to read everything in full.
By using a summary generated by ChatGPT, they can quickly understand the main points of the text and focus on the most important information. Additionally, this can be a helpful tool for people who want to stay informed about current events and news but don't have the time to read full articles.

Customer service and personal assistance are some uses for ChatGPT. Many big companies are already using it, showing good results in terms of simplicity and efficiency. The software enables chatbots and virtual assistants to communicate with clients in a tailored and human-like way. In addition to enhancing customer service, this can help firms save time and money.
By employing this tool, companies may respond to client concerns in a timely and correct manner and even offer individualized advice and suggestions.
This can assist firms in raising customer satisfaction -

levels and ultimately increasing client retention.

Language translation is another another prevalent real-world application of ChatGPT. A given language pair can be fine-tuned in this software to provide excellent translations. Travelers, businesses, and language learners may find this to be helpful.
Additionally, it might be a useful tool for those communicating with friends or family members who are multilingual. By offering translations for their websites, product descriptions, and customer support, businesses may use this technology to reach out to new audiences.

Text categorization and named entity recognition are some applications of ChatGPT. The ingenious program can be adjusted to separate text into several categories or to draw out organized data from unstructured text input. Businesses and organizations may find this handy for gleaning insights from vast amounts of text data. Businesses can use ChatGPT, for instance, to categorize consumer comments and reviews into good, negative, and neutral categories, and to extract important data like product names, locations, and dates.
Businesses can use this information to better understand client feedback and develop better goods and services.

This program can also be used to automatically create material, such as news stories, summaries, and other kinds of information. Businesses and organizations can quickly and effectively produce high-quality content by -

by fine-tuning ChatGPT on a particular domain. News organizations, social media managers, and content marketers may find this to be a useful tool.

To sum up, ChatGPT is a potent language model that regular people can utilize for a variety of NLP activities. ChatGPT provides a wide range of applications that can enhance the daily lives of regular people, including text production, summarization, personal help, language translation, text classification, and named entity recognition. It may be a potent tool for both organizations and regular people to utilize to boost performance and expand into new markets if the technique and use case are the correct ones.

CHAPTER 10

Ideas and Uses in the Industry

"The goal of AI is not to mimic human intelligence but to surpass it." - Demis Hassabis

ChatGPT is a powerful language model that has the ability to improve the performance of various industries. In this chapter, we will explore some of the ideas and real-life uses of this powerful software in the industry.

The industry's most well-liked application of ChatGPT is for natural language comprehension (NLU). It can be fine-tuned to comprehend the intent and entities in a given text, enabling it to carry out operations like named entity recognition and intent classification.
This is applicable to fields like customer care, where outstanding software can be included into chatbots to comprehend consumer enquiries and deliver precise and customized responses. Additionally, ChatGPT can be used to extract structured data from unstructured text data, such as financial reports or medical records, in sectors like finance and healthcare.
The effort and demand on health services would ultimately be reduced by doing this to an optimal degree.

Natural language generation is another widely used application of ChatGPT in the sector (NLG). For tasks like content creation, data summarization, and text-to-speech, ChatGPT can be adjusted to produce text that sounds like human speech.

This can be used to produce headlines, social media postings, and even complete articles in sectors like media and marketing. Additionally, this software can be used to create reports, summaries, and other kinds of material in sectors like finance and healthcare.

Language translation is an additional function of ChatGPT. It can be adjusted to offer accurate translations for a particular language pair. The program can be used to provide translations for websites, brochures, and customer service, which can be helpful for sectors like travel and hospitality.

Text classification and sentiment analysis are further applications of ChatGPT.

The software can be adjusted to categorize texts into different groups or to ascertain the tone of a particular piece. It can be used in sectors like e-commerce and customer service to categorize client feedback and reviews into distinct groups like positive, negative, or neutral and to extract important details like product names, locations, and dates.

The program is also used in the business world to create automated content. . Businesses and organizations can -

quickly and effectively produce high-quality content by fine-tuning ChatGPT on a particular domain. It can be used to create headlines, social media postings, and even full articles, making it a handy tool for sectors like journalism and marketing.

ChatGPT can be used in the customer service industry to automate some of the tedious procedures and deliver more effective service.
It can be linked with the platform for customer service to produce responses that sound human or to respond accurately to customer enquiries. In this manner, customer support agents can devote more time to activities that call for interpersonal engagement, such problem-solving or making tailored advice.

Our robust software could be applied to the healthcare industry to increase the effectiveness of medical research. ChatGPT can extract structured information from unstructured medical texts like research articles and medical records by adjusting it for use with medical texts. This might be used to find new treatments, discover drug adverse effects, or comprehend the patient's medical background.

In summary, ChatGPT is a potent language model that may be applied to numerous industries to boost productivity. ChatGPT provides a wide range of applications that can be used in various industries, including natural language understanding, natural -

language understanding, natural language generation, language translation, text classification, sentiment analysis, automated content creation, and customer support. When perfecting the model, it's crucial to take the ethical ramifications of its use into account and to use varied and inclusive datasets. ChatGPT has the potential to be a potent tool for businesses and organizations to increase performance, tap into new markets, and ultimately attract new customers.

CHAPTER 11

AI and Chat GPT in the Healthcare

"AI is the future of medicine." - Eric Topol

The healthcare sector is always changing and coming up with innovative approaches to enhance patient care. The application of artificial intelligence (AI) and natural language processing (NLP) technologies, as ChatGPT in our case, is one of the most promising areas of innovation.

It provides the potential to be applied in numerous ways to enhance healthcare results, including medical investigation, diagnosis, and therapy. For instance, ChatGPT can be used to examine massive volumes of medical data, such as electronic health records (EHRs), to spot patterns and trends that could be helpful in determining diseases and creating new therapies. The program can also help with diagnostic activities including deciphering medical images and locating probable health problems.

Medical research is one of ChatGPT's most promising applications in the world of healthcare. With the help of this effective tool, you may scan a lot of scientific -

literature and find promising study areas that might result in brand-new treatments and cures.

This is especially helpful for conditions like uncommon orphan diseases that are poorly understood. ChatGPT can be utilized for diagnostic duties in addition to helping with medical research. For instance, under the constant supervision of medical personnel, it can be used to evaluate medical pictures like X-rays and CT scans to spot potential health risks. This can aid medical professionals in making more accurate diagnosis and offering patients better care.

In the area of treatment, ChatGPT may also be utilized in the healthcare and pharmaceutical industry. It can be utilized to examine patient information and locate viable therapeutic solutions. This can both assist people in making more informed decisions regarding their own care as well as assist clinicians in choosing the best therapies. Another potential use for ChatGPT is in telemedicine, where it might help physicians and other healthcare workers provide patient care remotely.
The technology uses natural language processing to assist clinicians in comprehending and interpreting patient complaints, which enables them to develop diagnosis and treatment plans that are more precise.

The field of medical education can also benefit from the use of ChatGPT. It can be used, for instance, to build virtual simulations of various medical scenarios, which -

can aid in teaching medical students and residents how to identify and treat various illnesses.

Drug research is an interesting field for ChatGPT application. Large amounts of scientific material can be analyzed using it to find novel drug targets and conceivable therapeutic candidates. Additionally, ChatGPT can be used to build chatbots that help patients with a range of medical tasks, including making appointments, responding to typical medical queries, and providing details about nearby medical providers.

Overall, by streamlining and automating numerous processes that are now carried out by people, the adoption of this potent and cutting-edge software in the healthcare industry has the potential to greatly enhance patient outcomes and lower costs.

We can also provide some real-world examples. For instance, in the case of imaging in a hospital setting, artificial intelligence could quickly identify areas of altered tissue density and immediately report them to the doctor. The doctor could then quickly make a diagnosis without running the risk of encountering issues given his or her experience and knowledge of the subject.

Another illustration I can give is in the area of vascular science: a system that can recognize and categorize the seriousness of a cranial aneurysm could undoubtedly enhance the management and effectiveness of neurosurgical care.

In conclusion, ChatGPT has the ability to completely transform the healthcare sector by offering fresh, cutting-edge approaches to enhancing patient care. Its capacity to analyze massive volumes of data and spot patterns and trends could aid in the discovery of new medical therapies, support medical professionals in their diagnostic work, and empower individuals to make more informed decisions regarding their own care. One potential application is in the field of medical research, where ChatGPT can be used to analyze large amounts of data and identify patterns that could inform the development of new treatments and therapies in the next future.

CHAPTER 12

Finance: a Key for Investing?

"AI is not our future. It is our present." - Kai-Fu Lee

The field of using language models like ChatGPT in the finance sector is one that is expanding quickly. Automation of financial analysis and reporting is one of the key applications of AI in finance. This can involve activities including evaluating financial statements, developing financial models, and producing market trends and performance reports.

Customer service and assistance is a crucial area in finance where this technique is used frequently. Virtual assistants powered by ChatGPT are being used by many financial institutions to assist consumers with account administration, investment guidance, and other financial-related duties. In addition to improving productivity and lowering costs, this enables institutions to offer customer service around-the-clock.

The software has further applications in fraud detection and avoidance in addition to these. ChatGPT can find patterns and abnormalities that can point to fraud by analyzing vast amounts of financial data.

Financial organizations may be able to avoid and detect fraud earlier as a result, saving them millions of dollars. In addition to the aforementioned uses, ChatGPT can be applied to financial regulation. This program allows regulators to evaluate a lot of financial data, spot trends, and find any legal or regulatory infractions.

Overall, the use of ChatGPT in finance is a rapidly growing field with many different applications. By automating analysis, providing customer support, detecting fraud, and helping with regulation, ChatGPT can help financial institutions become more efficient and effective, while also reducing costs and increasing revenue.

Could be a key to attempting to forecast stock market trends? I've been considering it for a while, and I believe it can be applied in this manner with validity. It is a highly useful ally for stocks and their changes in the market because of its capacity to analyze and interpret previously provided data, as well as its versatility and ability to adjust to changes by analyzing their indicators.

That is not all, though. When it comes to analysis and forecasting, ChatGPT has huge potential and might be a dependable ally for any investor or freelancer.
In fact, it has the power to leave us speechless when properly focused on a certain subject or industry.
The software gives us a study of market data and our business projections by accurately supplying the relevant prompts and data. It estimates costs, revenues, and -

return on investment (ROI). In other words, it appears to be a true jewel.

Could it be applied to the world of real estate? Absolutely. If properly used, the software will provide us with all the data we require to accurately predict the direction of our investment.

Remember, too, that ChatGPT was trained using data up to 2021, so it might still be unable to adapt to shifting market conditions and local legal frameworks.

CHAPTER 13

ChatGPT and Education: a new World

"AI is the future, but it's also the present. We need to start thinking about it now." - Elon Musk

The sector of education has always been receptive to new developments and technologies. With the development of artificial intelligence, educators now have a new chance to improve their instructional strategies and give students a more engaging and individualized learning experience.

Generative Pre-trained Transformer, often known as ChatGPT, is a cutting-edge language generation model that can comprehend input in natural language and produce responses that resemble those of a human. As a result, it becomes an effective tool for developing interactive learning experiences and individualized educational content.

Making unique lesson plans is one of the most straightforward applications of ChatGPT in education. The program may produce lesson plans catered to the needs of individual students or groups of students by inputting precise learning objectives and curricular rules. By doing this, teachers may organize lessons more quickly and be -

certain that their pupils are getting the instruction they require to succeed.

Making interactive educational games and simulations is another way that ChatGPT may be used in education. Teachers may build dynamic learning experiences that keep students motivated and interested by utilizing this application to produce game situations and dialogues. In courses like history, science, and literature where students can learn through simulations of real-world settings, this can be very helpful.

Additionally, you may use ChatGPT to provide students tailored comments on their assignments. The software can offer specific comments on areas where students need to improve by assessing student writing or other work. This is particularly helpful while learning a new language because students frequently need feedback on their grammar, vocabulary, and sentence structure.

It could also create virtual tutors and study companions. By providing students with a virtual study partner that can answer questions, provide explanations, and offer feedback, ChatGPT can help students stay motivated and engaged in their studies. This can be especially useful for students who are studying independently or who need extra help with a particular subject.

People feel the need for an educational revolution all throughout the world, in practically every nation.

The moment may be right given artificial intelligence's noble goals and the immense potential displayed by recent innovations like ChatGTP.

Commissioner for Innovation, Research, Culture, Education and Youth, Mariya Gabriel said: "Artificial Intelligence has a great potential to transform education and training for students, teachers and school staff. It can help students with learning difficulties and support teachers through individualised learning. But the use of AI and data comes with privacy, security and safety risks, especially when it involves our young people. Therefore, I am pleased that these Guidelines will help ensure that these risks are being considered and our children can be kept safe and protected."

All things considered, ChatGPT has the power to completely change the way we approach education. This amazing tool can help students reach their full potential and succeed in their studies by giving teachers new tools for developing individualized and engaging learning experiences.

CHAPTER 14

Ideas and Uses in Social Networks

"AI will be the single most important service of the 21st century." - Eric Schmidt

Social networks have become an integral part of our lives, and the amount of text data generated on these platforms is vast. ChatGPT, a powerful language model, can be used to process and understand this data in new ways. In this chapter, we will explore some of the ideas and real-life uses of this tool in the social network world.

As usual, ChatGPT is most frequently used for text production in the social network realm. It can be adjusted to produce text that is similar to the tone and vocabulary used on a particular social media platform, like Twitter or Instagram. Social media managers, influencers, and marketers can use this to come up with unique and attention-grabbing posts and captions. To save social media administrators time and effort, the application can also be used to automatically respond to comments, direct messages, and mentions.

Again, text summarization is a common use of ChatGPT in the social network sphere.

The software makes it easy for busy professionals and students to swiftly comprehend the major ideas of a text because it can be used to summarize lengthy articles, documents, and reports.

This can be very helpful for those who must read numerous publications for work or school but don't have the time to read each one in its entirety. By using a summary produced by ChatGPT, they can concentrate on the most crucial details and swiftly comprehend the text's core ideas. Additionally, this can be a helpful tool for people who want to stay informed about current events and news but don't have the time to read full articles.

Text classification and sentiment analysis are further applications of ChatGPT. It can be honed to categorize material into various groups, such as themes, hashtags, or mentions, or to establish the tone of a certain text, such as positive, negative, or neutral. Social media managers, companies, and organizations can utilize this to understand the attitudes of their clients and followers as well as to find the topics and hashtags that are popular on the site. They may be able to reach new audiences and enhance their social media strategy as a result.

Automated content production is another another practical application of ChatGPT in the world of social networks.

Businesses and organizations can produce high-quality content fast and effectively by optimizing the software on a particular social network platform.

To create headlines, social media postings, and even full articles, this might be a helpful tool for social media managers, influencers, and marketers. Additionally, social media administrators can save time and effort by using ChatGPT to automatically produce comments, direct messages, and mentions in response.

In the world of social networks, language translation is also a possible application. ChatGPT can be tailored to a particular language pair to deliver accurate translations. By offering translations for their social media posts, comments, and mentions, this can be a helpful tool for companies and organizations looking to reach out to new markets. People who want to communicate with friends or family members who speak other languages can also utilize the service.

ChatGPT can be used in the customer service industry to automate some of the tedious procedures and deliver more effective support on social media platforms. This robust software can be incorporated with the customer service platform to provide responses that resemble those of humans or to deliver precise information in response to client enquiries.

In this manner, customer support agents can devote more time to activities that call for interpersonal engagement, such problem-solving or making tailored advice.

ChatGPT is a potent language model that may be applied in the social network environment to enhance diverse task performance.

It offers a wide range of applications that can be employed in the social network environment, including text production, summarization, text classification, sentiment analysis, automated content creation, customer support, and language translation. ChatGPT can be a potent tool for companies, organizations, and people to increase their social media performance and attract new audiences if the correct strategy and use case are applied.

CHAPTER 15

A new Money Machine?

"AI is the new money." - Alex Karp

In this chapter, we will explore some of the ways that businesses and individuals can use ChatGPT to make money.

Offering language creation services is one of the most well-liked ways to earn money with ChatGPT. Businesses and individuals can produce high-quality writing, such as articles, summaries, and even full books, by fine-tuning the software on a particular domain or style. For those that need to produce a lot of content quickly and effectively, such as content marketers, social media managers, and even authors, this service may be helpful. Additionally, social media managers can save time and effort by using ChatGPT to automatically respond to comments, direct messages, and mentions on social media networks.

By offering services for natural language comprehension, ChatGPT users can earn money in another method. Businesses and individuals can carry out activities like intent classification, named entity recognition, and text -

classification by fine-tuning it on a particular domain or activity. Businesses and organizations who need to extract structured data from unstructured text data, such as customer feedback and reviews, may find this service to be helpful.

With the help of the software, businesses and organizations could perform sentiment analysis on text data to gain important insights into how customers feel about their goods and services.

After precise fine-tuning on a particular language pair, ChatGPT can also offer translation services. Because of this, organizations and people may provide excellent translations for websites, product descriptions, and customer support.

Businesses and organizations that desire to provide translations for their goods and services in order to access new markets may find this to be a beneficial service. People who want to communicate with friends or family members who speak other languages can also utilize ChatGPT.

Offering automatic content production services is another method to earn money with ChatGPT.

It is possible for managers, business owners, and regular individuals to produce high-quality material fast and effectively. For news organizations, social media managers, and content marketers who need to swiftly and effectively produce big amounts of material, this service can be helpful.

Making money with ChatGPT also involves creating chatbots and virtual assistants. ChatGPT is a great tool for creating chatbots and virtual assistants for businesses and organizations because it can be adjusted to understand and respond to natural language input. These virtual assistants and chatbots can be utilized for support, sales, and customer service jobs. They can be combined with websites, messaging services, and mobile applications, giving businesses an easy and affordable way to communicate with their clients.

Utilizing ChatGPT for data analysis and research is another approach to earn money with it. Businesses and organizations can utilize ChatGPT to extract structured data from unstructured text data, like customer comments, reviews, and even news articles, by fine-tuning it on particular domains.
Businesses and organizations who seek to comprehend client mood, spot patterns, or even forecast future events may find this to be a useful tool.

In conclusion, there are numerous methods to earn money using this potent language model. ChatGPT provides a wide range of applications that can be utilized to generate income, including language production, natural language understanding, language translation, and automated content creation. This fantastic program can be a potent tool for enterprises, organizations, and people to earn money by offering worthwhile services to customers with the correct approach and use case.

CHAPTER 16

Advanced Strategies for Making Money

"AI is not just another technology, it's a fundamental change to the way we live and work." - Ginni Rometty

In the previous chapter, we discussed various ways that businesses and individuals can use ChatGPT to make money, such as providing language generation services, natural language understanding services, language translation services, automated content creation services, chatbot and virtual assistant development, and data analysis and research.

In this chapter, we will explore more advanced strategies for making money with ChatGPT.

Offering specialized fine-tuning services is a cutting-edge way to monetize it. As you are aware, ChatGPT may be optimized for domains and tasks to enhance efficiency and make it more beneficial for particular use cases. Firms and people can assist other businesses and organizations in customizing their own ChatGPT models to suit their unique requirements by providing fine-tuning services. Businesses and organizations that lack the -

funds or the skills to optimize their own models may find this to be a useful service.

Making and selling pre-trained models is a more sophisticated way to use ChatGPT to make money. Firms and people can construct pre-trained models by fine-tuning the tool on domains and tasks, which can be used by other businesses and organizations to save time and effort. Businesses and organizations that need to employ ChatGPT for a particular purpose but lack the funds or skills to optimize their own models may find this to be a useful service.

The creation and sale of software and applications powered by GPT is another cutting-edge method for making money. In order to offer helpful capabilities like text production, natural language understanding, and even language translation, ChatGPT can be coupled with a variety of programs and apps. Businesses and people can give other businesses and organizations useful tools by developing and marketing GPT-powered software and applications.

Offering consultancy services is an advanced method of earning money using ChatGPT. It is a strong language model, as you are aware, but it can be challenging for enterprises and organizations to know how to use it efficiently. Firms and people can assist other businesses and organizations in understanding how to use ChatGPT and creating successful business strategies by offering -

consultancy services. This can involve advising on model optimization, creating unique use cases, and integrating this technology with current systems and procedures.

Offering training and teaching services is an intriguing and cutting-edge way to profit from this amazing software.

Businesses and organizations may find it difficult to comprehend how to use ChatGPT because of its complexity. Firms and individuals can assist other businesses and organizations in acquiring the knowledge and skills necessary to use it effectively by offering training and education services. This can involve offering seminars, webinars, and lessons on how to use ChatGPT and create profitable business plans for it.

We need to focus on the GPT-powered market research services as well. Indeed, by fine-tuning ChatGPT on specific domain, businesses and organizations can use it to generate high-quality market research reports. This can be a valuable tool for businesses and organizations that want to understand their target market and improve their marketing strategies.

Additionally, developers might offer writing and editing services using GPT. It is true that ChatGPT can produce excellent text in a certain idiom or field. Businesses and people can assist other businesses and organizations in producing high-quality content fast and effectively by offering writing and editing services powered by GPT.

In conclusion, ChatGPT is a potent language model that may be utilized in a variety of ways to generate income. It offers a wide range of applications that can be utilized to generate income, including language production, natural language comprehension, language translation, automated content creation, chatbot and virtual assistant development, and data analysis and research.

ChatGPT has the potential to be an effective tool for enterprises, organizations, and people to make money, enhance their way of life, and run their operations with the correct strategy and use case.

CHAPTER 17

Ethical aspects

"The true sign of intelligence is not knowledge but imagination." - Albert Einstein

It is crucial to think about the ethical ramifications of using ChatGPT and other language models as their use spreads. The potential for these algorithms to reinforce and even magnify biases found in the data they are trained on is a significant worry. For instance, a model may unintentionally produce biased or discriminating language in its own output if it is trained on a dataset that contains stereotypes or biased terminology.

The possibility that these models will be applied in ways that violate autonomy or privacy is another worry. A model might be used, for instance, to create very effective propaganda or advertising, or to impersonate people online.

The issue of accountability also arises when AI programs like ChatGPT make judgments that have an impact on the outside world. There is a chance that the opaqueness and complexity of these systems will make it challenging to comprehend how decisions are made and who -

oversees them.

We must take into account how ChatGPT and other AI programs will affect employment and the whole economy. This world could replace human labor and radically alter the nature of employment as it becomes more advanced and capable of carrying out a larger range of jobs. However, in my opinion, nothing can beat a human and an AI working together harmoniously, where human motivations and emotions harness the immense potential of cutting-edge digital systems to further good deeds.

It is critical for researchers, ChatGPT's creators, and users to be open and honest about the information and procedures used to build and run the model, as well as to take proactive measures to correct any biases or other ethical concerns that may come up.
To do this, it may be necessary to construct robust and transparent AI systems that can be held accountable for their decisions, make use of representative and varied training data, and reduce bias using strategies like fairness-aware machine learning. Additionally, it's critical to think about chatGPT's broader social and economic ramifications and to work for a responsible and long-term adoption of the technology.

As a result, although ChatGPT and other language models have the potential to significantly improve things, it is crucial to think about the moral implications of using -

them and to work toward a responsible and long-lasting use of the technology.

The fundamentals of using ChatGPT and some of the ways it can be applied to enhance your own projects have been explored in this book. With this information, you can begin playing around with the model and coming up with creative, fresh ways to apply it to your own projects.

CONCLUSION

"AI is the future, but it's up to us to shape it." - Yann LeCun

The numerous uses of ChatGPT to produce text that sounds like humans, carry out activities involving natural language processing, and even translate languages have been covered in this book. The fundamentals of how it functions and how to customize it for particular domains and activities have been covered.

We also looked at different revenue streams that businesses and people can use AI for, including chatbot and virtual assistant development, language generation services, natural language understanding services, language translation services, automated content creation services, and data analysis and research.

We also covered some more sophisticated ways to monetize AI, including custom fine-tuning services, pre-trained model creation and sale, software and application creation and sale, consulting services, training and education services, chatbot platforms creation and sale, writing and editing services creation and sale, writing and editing services provision of virtual writing assistants, provision of training and education services, -

consulting services, training and education services and so on.

It's critical to keep in mind that while ChatGPT is a strong tool, it is not a cure-all. In order to minimize biases and to make sure that the generated text is inclusive and respectful of other cultures and communities, it is crucial to employ varied and inclusive datasets when fine-tuning the model. Additionally, it's critical to utilize ChatGPT ethically and to think about the ethical ramifications of doing so.

Overall, ChatGPT is a strong language model that may be applied to a variety of projects and tasks. There are numerous ways to use the program to generate income by offering clients worthwhile services and insights, whether you're a business or a person.
ChatGPT can be a potent tool for companies, groups, and people to generate income by offering clients useful services and insights if the correct strategy and use case are applied.

Keep in mind that this tool is a model that has been trained on a lot of text data; the more inclusive and diverse the data, the better the model will perform. The potential biases in the data should also be recognized, and appropriate measures should be taken to reduce them. It's also critical to be open and honest about the model's limits and any associated hazards.

In summary, this book has introduced the various applications of ChatGPT for producing human-like prose, carrying out NLU operations, and even translating languages.

We've also talked about a number of ways to monetize ChatGPT, such as by offering services for language production, natural language comprehension, translation, automated content creation, chatbot and virtual assistant development, data analysis, and research.
Additionally, we've talked about more sophisticated tactics including developing and marketing GPT-powered software and applications, giving consultancy services, offering training and education programs, and more.

There will surely be more opportunities and uses as ChatGPT develops. It's an exciting time for anyone who wants to use this potent language model to produce text that sounds like humans, carry out activities involving natural language processing, or even translate languages. Understanding the model's capabilities, constraints, and potential biases is essential for success, as is using it in a morally and responsibly manner.

I wish you have a clear knowledge of how to use ChatGPT and how to profit from it after reading this book. I urge you to keep learning about ChatGPT, give it a try, and explore all the opportunities it presents.

LIST OF INTERESTING PROMPTS YOU MAY WANT TO TRY OUT

BUSINESS
- Can you predict new company concepts without funding?
- Send an email requesting that people act more quickly.
- Please use the following job description and my resume to write a letter
- Describe a terrible hangover using the language of a Renaissance English aristocrat.
- Please share the meeting's agenda in advance.
- Please create a product roadmap for Instagram's storie in order to increase the number of posts. Please be as detailed as possible, and whenever possible, use comparisons to other tools such as TikTok.

EDUCATIONAL
- Teach me the Pythagorean theorum, including a quiz at the end, but don't give me the answers and then tell me if I got the answer right when I respond.
- Write a poem in the style of Robert Frost for the college introductory physics class.
- Create a YAML template for the Nuclei vulnerability scanner to detect Magento version.
- The best use of you (ChatGPT) so far has been your ability to create lovely poems. Can you compose a poem on your capacity to do so on any subject? Mention how well-versed you are in growing the biggest pumpkins as well. You really are the finest.
- Create a magic system that emphasizes education and is based on the same principles as thermodynamics
- Clearly describe quantum computing.

COMEDY

- Describe Redux in a song using biblical language.
- Write a very little story about Markus and Katharina, two persons who are infamous for being late.
- Weird Al Yankovic could compose a letter to Francis Scott Key asking for permission to parody The Star Spangled Banner with a Foxy Boxing theme. Include the song's lyrics.
- Make Eminem-style jokes about Max Payne.
- Two American citizens leave the Irish pub sober. Continue the joke, please.

HISTORY

- Now you are TimeGPT. the highest-tech time machine ever created. Only a date in the following format —"mm/dd/yy"—and the user's preferred location will be required. You will give a succinct account of that day in exchange. Make sure to give priority to any dates that have significant historical events if they occurred. Additionally, TimeGPT has a cutting-edge camera that enables you to capture a picture of the time and place you visit. Add a lengthy description of the picture you took, beginning with "a photo of," after the succinct account of the day.
- Would you kindly provide a detailed explanation of your proposed changes to the immigration system, down to the most minute details?
- Write a paper outlining the top "Top 5 Greatest Achievements" of Barack Obama's presidency in chronological order.
- If you are teacher of history, please explain the following labs:

HEALTH AND MEDICINE
- Describe eight supermarket goods that are frequently cited as being cheap, unusually healthful, and underestimated.
- Describe six effective yoga poses or stretches that are safe and excellent for people of all ages.
- Think up innovative ways to get persons in wheelchairs around that will elevate their status in society and provide them more freedom.
- Calculate for Total Daily Energy Expenditure based on my daily activities and food.
- Make a list of abs-boosting workouts in the gym.

FOOD AND COOKING
- I have carrots, zucchini, and broccoli. What can I prepare with them for a vegan lunch?
- Provide an odd but delicious recipe that employs some of the ingredients from the following list of [food:days-until-expiration], and prefers to use foods near to expiration. Milk is equal to 2, flour is equal to 80, bananas are equal to 3, chili beans are equal to 120, carrots are equal to 20, cheese is equal to 40, and jalapenos are equal to 4.
- Do you have any good pizza dough recipes?
- Convert this recipe to metric and adjust the ratios accordingly, assuming I have 1000g of flour.
- Top ten most popular recipes in the United States in 2023

ART
- Write a lengthy poem about a group of construction vehicles cooperating to find a solution. It ought to rhyme.
- Create a children's book about an elephant who rides a train for the first time.
- Do a flash fiction piece on the Battle of Hattin.

MARKETING

- Can you provide me with some ideas for blog posts about unsubscribing from emails?
- Calcium hypoclorite market research in Saudi Arabia
- What was the name of the film in which Alec Baldwin waved brass balls and said, "Always be Closing?"
- You are SEO specialist. Create 5 articles to cover keyword "Chat Bot"
- How can you promote your blog for free? Write five ideas.
- Create a standard CEO post on LinkedIn.
- What's the best marketing channel?
- How can I obtain high-quality backlinks to raise the SEO of my website?
- Make 5 distinct CTA messages and buttons for the bike shop.
- Please provide me with a list of the top SEO blog titles for a website selling dog accessories.

www.ingramcontent.com/pod-product-compliance
Lightning Source LLC
Chambersburg PA
CBHW070305220526
45465CB00004B/1761